EARTH MATERIALS AND SYSTEMS

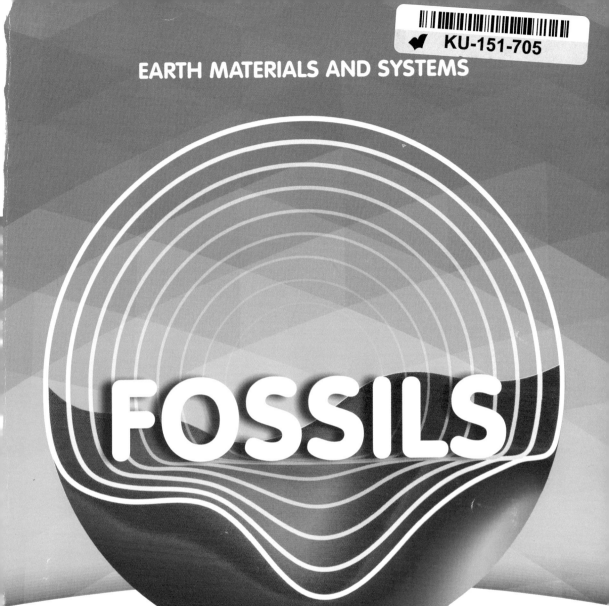

FOSSILS

by Keli Sipperley

raintree
a Capstone company — publishers for children

Raintree is an imprint of Capstone Global Library Limited, a company incorporated in England and Wales having its registered office at 264 Banbury Road, Oxford, OX2 7DY – Registered company number: 6695582

www.raintree.co.uk
myorders@raintree.co.uk

Edited by Charly Haley
Designed by Jake Nordby
Original illustrations © Capstone Global Library Limited 2022
Production by Joshua Olson
Originated by Capstone Global Library Ltd
Printed and bound in India

978 1 3982 0415 7 (hardback)
978 1 3982 0408 9 (paperback)

British Library Cataloguing in Publication Data
A full catalogue record for this book is available from the British Library.

Acknowledgements
We would like to thank the following for permission to reproduce photographs: iStockphoto: _curly_, 13, benedek, 25, jdjana, 27, ScottOrr, cover; Shutterstock Images: Alizada Studios, 9, Bjoern Wylezich, 12, Danny Ye, 16-17, EcoPrint, 19, gob_cu, 23, Hugh K Telleria, 5, Jaroslav Moravcik, 10, paleontologist natural, 20, Russ Vance, 28, steve estvanik, 6, Xolodan, 15. Design elements: Shutterstock Images

CONTENTS

Words in **bold** are in the glossary.

What are fossils?

Fossils are the remains of living things that died long ago. Plants and animals became fossils. Some fossils are tiny. Some are as big as a bus. Each is like a puzzle piece. Together they teach us about the past.

Fossils form over millions of years. Many things that made them are no longer alive. Dinosaurs made the largest fossils ever found. They lived more than 65 million years ago.

Some museums
show fossils.

HOW RARE WAS T-REX?

Fossils are hard like rocks. But they are not ordinary rocks. One might show a footprint. Another might show a leaf.

Other fossils are shaped like the things they came from. Some are shaped like bones. Some are shaped like teeth.

There are different types of fossils. Body fossils are one type. These come from hard parts of dead plants or animals. The soft parts do not become fossils. They break down too fast.

Bones can become body fossils. Teeth and shells can too. Tree branches can become body fossils.

A nest fossil

Trace fossils are another type of fossil. These are not from the bodies of dead things. They come from things that living animals made.

Footprints and scratches can become trace fossils. Nests can too. **Scientists** have found dinosaur poo. It is another trace fossil. They study it to learn what dinosaurs ate.

Amber fossils are another type of fossil. These are made with tree **resin**. An insect falls into this sticky stuff and gets trapped. The resin hardens. It becomes a fossil. This happens to plants too.

Where are fossils?

Fossils are rare. Only one bone in a billion becomes a fossil. A dead thing must be buried fast to do this. It must not break down.

Fossils are found all over the world. They are in deserts. They are in the ocean floor. They are on mountains.

Whale bones have been found in deserts. They are millions of years old. They show us that Earth has changed a lot. Some deserts were once oceans.

The best fossils are found where water flowed. The water pushed the bones deep into the ground.

How do things become fossils?

A buried bone is not a fossil straight away. It becomes one over time. This can take millions of years.

Some fossils form in ice. Some form in tar. But most are in rocks. A dead plant or animal gets buried in sand or mud. The sand or mud hardens. This makes rocks. The plant or animal becomes a fossil.

Fossils can get buried deeper over time. So how do we find them? People dig to find fossils. Scientists work together. They dig in an area. They study what they find.

Sometimes wind and water help. They wear down rocks. They wash dust away. Then it is easier to see fossils.

Why are fossils important?

Fossils help us learn about the past. They tell us about life on Earth. The oldest fossils are from **bacteria**. They are billions of years old. Dinosaur fossils are up to 243 million years old. The oldest human remains are 315,000 years old.

Fossils show us animals and plants that are no longer living. Teeth show how animals ate. Leg bones show how they moved. Nests show how they raised their young.

Fossils show us how Earth has changed. Alligator fossils have been found in the Arctic. Today, the Arctic is too cold for alligators. The fossils tell us the Arctic was warmer a long time ago.

Scientists study fossils. Sometimes only one bone is found. These scientists work out what animal it came from. They look at where the bone was found. They check how old it is.

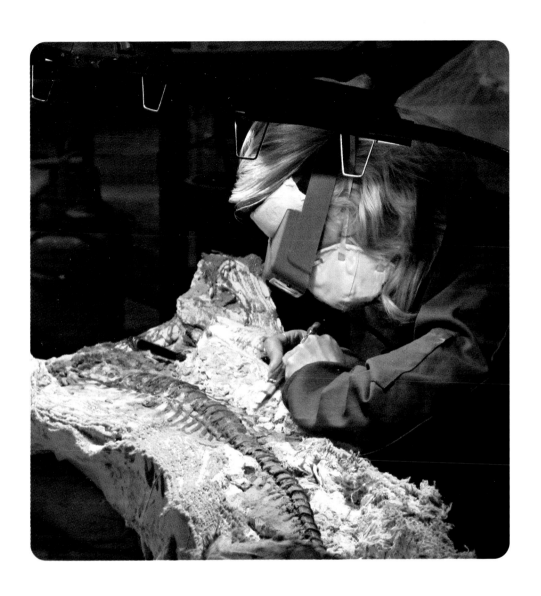

Sometimes many bones are found.

Scientists put the pieces together.

People also use fossils for fuel. **Coal**, **oil** and **natural gas** are made from them. These are called fossil fuels. They took millions of years to form. People burn them for heat and electricity.

But people are using these fuels faster than new fossils form. The fuels will run out. So scientists are finding other ways to make electricity. One way is with solar power. It uses sunlight.

Petrol is made from fossil fuels.

Fossil clue:

Finding fossils is exciting. Some show dinosaurs fighting. Others show fish eating a dinosaur. Some show penguins as tall as adult humans!

Today, people write things down. They take photos. These give us a **record** of life on Earth. But there are no photos from millions of years ago. The history from that time is a puzzle. Fossils help us put the puzzle together.

Glossary

bacteria microscopic living things

coal black substance formed from the remains of ancient plants

natural gas gas found underground that is used for heating and cooling

oil thick, greasy liquid that burns easily and does not mix with water

record facts about what people or other living things have done

resin sticky substance produced by some trees

scientists people who study nature and other things by testing and measuring

Find out more

Books

Fossil (DK Eyewitness), DK (DK Children, 2017)

Fossils (Rock On!), Chris Oxlade (Raintree, 2017)

How Long Does It Take to Make a Fossil?
(How Long Does It Take?), Emily Hudd
(Raintree, 2020)

Websites

**www.bbc.co.uk/bitesize/topics/z9bbkqt/articles/
z2ym2p3**

Learn more about how fossils are made.

**www.dkfindout.com/uk/dinosaurs-and-
prehistoric-life**

Find out more about dinosaurs and prehistoric life.

Index